VIDEO GAMES

FROM CONCEPT TO CONSUMER

BY KEVIN CUNNINGHAM

CHILDREN'S PRESS®

An Imprint of Scholastic Inc.
New York Toronto London Auckland Sydney
Mexico City New Delhi Hong Kong
Danbury, Connecticut

CONTENT CONSULTANT
Dr. John C. Hart, Professor of Computer Science, University of Illinois at Urbana–Champaign

PHOTOGRAPHS © 2014: age footstock/Joe Fox: 28 bottom; Alamy Images: 44 (adiseshan shankar), 17 (B.O'Kane), 10 left (ClassicStock), 24, 25 bottom (epa european pressphoto agency b.v.), 4 left, 14 (GOIMAGES), 48 (Henrik Kettunen), 31 (Iain Masterton), 9 (INTERFOTO), 18 bottom (Joe Fox), 23 (keith morris), 29 (M Itani), 3, 15 (pumkinpie), 53 (Ringo Chiu/Zuma Press), 27 (ZUMA Press, Inc.); AP Images: 46 (Activision), 22 (dapd), 5 left, 41 (Disney), 43 (Elaine Thompson), 25 top (Kyodo), 58 (Microsoft), 59 (PRNewsFoto/ Sony Computer Entertainment America LLC), 57 (Richard Drew), 42 (Richard Lam, CP), 54 (Supergiant Games), 18 top, 30 (Ted S. Warren), 5 right, 49 (Warner Bros./DC Comics/ dapd); Courtesy of Casey O'Donnell: 38; Courtesy of the Computer History Museum/Gift of Hewlett-Packard Company: 8; Corbis Images: 52 (Liz Hafalia/San Francisco Chronicle), 13 (Ralf-Finn Hestoft), 45 (TWPhoto); DigiPen Institute of Technology: 50, 51; Getty Images: 20 (Daniel Boczarski), 16 (Gamma-Rapho), 32 (Ryan Anson/AFP), 35 (YOSHIKAZU TSUNO/ AFP); Courtesy of IS3D-Online, LLC: 39; iStockphoto/Chris Schmidt: 36; Landov/CHRISTINNE MUSCHI/Reuters: 37; Media Bakery: 6; Newscom: 34 (Jens Kalaene/dpa/picture-alliance), 19 (JOCELYN WILLIAMS KRT), 55 (MCT), 56 (ulrich niehoff Image Broker); Superstock, Inc.: 4 right, 26 (Iain Masterton/age fotostock), cover (Ingo Schulz/imagebroker.net), 28 top (Science and Society), 40 (Ton Koene/age fotostock); The Granger Collection: 10 right; The Image Works: 12 (St. Petersburg Times), 11 (Sven Simon/ullstein bild).

LIBRARY OF CONGRESS CATALOGING-IN-PUBLICATION DATA
Cunningham, Kevin, 1966–
  Video games : from concept to consumer / by Kevin Cunningham.
    p. cm. — (Calling all Innovators : A Career for You)
  Includes bibliographical references and index.
  ISBN 978-0-531-26523-9 (lib. bdg.) — ISBN 978-0-531-22011-5 (pbk.)
1. Video games industry — History — Juvenile literature. 2. Video games — History — Juvenile literature. 3. Video games — Design — Vocational guidance — Juvenile literature. I. Title.
  HD9993.E452C86 2013
  794.8023 — dc23   2012034208

All rights reserved. Published in 2014 by Children's Press, an imprint of Scholastic Inc.
Printed in the United States of America 113

SCHOLASTIC, CHILDREN'S PRESS, and associated logos are trademarks and/or registered trademarks of Scholastic Inc.

1 2 3 4 5 6 7 8 9 10 R 23 22 21 20 19 18 17 16 15 14

S

cience, technology, engineering, arts, and math are the fields that drive innovation. Whether they are finding ways to make our lives easier or developing the latest entertainment, the people who work in these fields are changing the world for the better. Do you have what it takes to join the ranks of today's greatest innovators? Read on to discover whether video game design is a career for you.

TABLE *of* CONTENTS

The Nintendo Game Boy popularized portable video games.

Angry Birds *is one of the most popular games on tablet computers.*

Texture artists create the interesting surfaces of video game characters such as this enemy from Epic Mickey 2.

Batman: Arkham City's incredible graphics helped make it a huge hit.

Around 40 percent of all video game players are female.

CHAPTER ONE

GAME ON

What would you like to do today? You could take control of a starship and blast off to explore a faraway galaxy. Or maybe you would rather travel back in time to fight in one of history's most famous wars. If you prefer something a little less dangerous, you could try throwing the game-winning pass in this year's Super Bowl. While it might seem impossible, you can do all this from the comfort of your own living room.

Video games are one of today's most popular pastimes. Millions of people around the world own home game consoles and handheld systems. Others play video games on cell phones or computers. But it wasn't long ago that video games didn't exist at all.

MAJOR CONSOLE LAUNCHES*

1977	1985	1995	1996	2001
Atari 2600	Nintendo Entertainment System	Sony PlayStation	Nintendo 64	Microsoft Xbox

*North American release dates

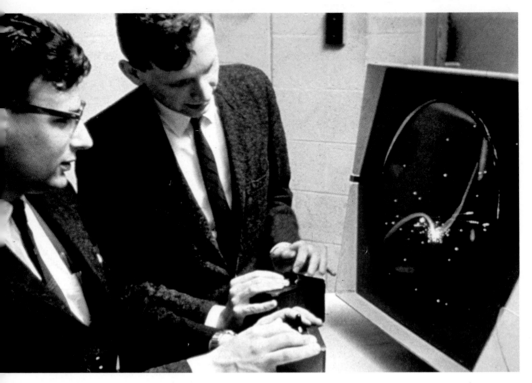

The original version of Spacewar! *was played on a circular screen.*

EARLY INNOVATORS

It all started with a simple game of tic-tac-toe. In 1952, A. S. Douglas, a student at Cambridge University in Great Britain, designed a tic-tac-toe game called *OXO* on Electronic Delay Storage Automatic Calculator (EDSAC), an early computer. EDSAC wasn't like today's computers. It was a one-of-a-kind machine that took up an entire room. As a result, *OXO* was never available to the public.

In the early 1960s, a group of programmers at the Massachusetts Institute of Technology developed a two-player game called *Spacewar!* Each player was given control of a spaceship, and the goal was to shoot the other player's ship. Versions of *Spacewar!* were created to run on several different types of computers, and the game quickly found a following among college-aged gamers around the country.

KING PONG

By the early 1970s, companies such as Magnavox and Atari had begun creating simple video games for the general public. In 1972, the Magnavox Odyssey was released. It was the first home video game console. Designed by engineer Ralph Baer, it allowed users to play simple interactive TV versions of table tennis, volleyball, checkers, soccer, and hockey.

At about the same time, Allan Alcorn was using his imagination and skills to design the electronic arcade tennis game he called *Pong*. The game, produced by Atari, was an immediate hit. According to Alcorn, part of the game's success was how easy it was to play. Even though the first players were not familiar with video games, *Pong* did not require any instructions. Atari released a home version of *Pong* for TV in 1975. Like the arcade version, it was a huge success.

Atari titled its game Pong *because the term Ping-Pong was already trademarked.*

Families once gathered closely around televisions so they could see the tiny screens.

EYES ON THE SCREEN

All video games, from the earliest experiments to the latest blockbusters, need some kind of screen to display their graphics. Because computer monitors and televisions did not become common until the mid-20th century, video games could not have existed any earlier than they did.

CATHODE-RAY TUBES

Early screens relied on large, heavy devices called cathode-ray tubes (CRTs) to produce images. Beginning in the 1990s, other technology such as liquid crystal display (LCD) and plasma screens became more popular. This allowed screens to be lighter, thinner, and more portable.

Color televisions were considered high-end luxury items when they were first released.

Most modern television screens offer a wider shape than earlier models did.

COLOR TELEVISION

The earliest televisions were sold in the late 1920s. They had small screens and could only display low-quality black-and-white images. The first color TVs were released in the 1950s, but they were considered a luxury item. It was not until the late 1960s that color TVs became common. Without this development, the colorful, realistic video game graphics of today would be impossible.

HIGH DEFINITION

Today, video screens range from small smartphone displays to huge, wall-mounted TVs. They offer colorful, detailed images that look just like real life. As screens have improved over time, video game designers have taken advantage of the new technology to improve their games' graphics. ✳

INSERT COIN

Though home consoles such as the Odyssey and Pong had a following, the real video game action during the late 1970s and early 1980s was in coin-operated arcade machines.

In 1980, the Japanese game company Namco released *Pac-Man*. Designed by Toru Iwatani, the arcade game was based on the idea of eating. Players controlled a round character with a big mouth and attempted to eat all of the dots in a level while avoiding a team of ghosts. *Pac-Man* surpassed even the hit video game *Space Invaders* in popularity. It was so huge that it inspired music, clothing, and a Saturday morning cartoon.

During the late 1970s and early 1980s, video game fans gathered around arcade machines and tried to beat each other's high scores on the latest games.

TOMOHIRO NISHIKADO

Japanese game designer Tomohiro Nishikado's 1978 arcade hit *Space Invaders* was one of the very first shooting games. It also pioneered the now common game features such as multiple lives, saved scores, and continuous background music. *Space Invaders* was so popular in Japan that the country suffered a coin shortage! Nishikado designed the entire game by himself, from its graphics and sound effects to the actual **hardware** of the arcade machine.

COLORFUL MARQUEE
ADVERTISES THE GAME'S TITLE

BUILT-IN MONITOR

PLAYERS INSERT COINS INTO THE
SLOTS OF ARCADE MACHINES

SUPER MARIO WORLD WAS THE FIRST ENTRY IN THE MARIO SERIES FOR THE SUPER NINTENDO ENTERTAINMENT SYSTEM.

As a child, Shigeru Miyamoto dreamed of becoming a puppeteer, but he decided to go into game design after playing Space Invaders.

BRINGING IT HOME

During the early 1980s, home consoles such as Atari's Video Computer System, Mattel's Intellivision, and Coleco's ColecoVision allowed people to play their favorite arcade games at home. But by the middle of the decade, these systems had decreased in popularity. The home video game industry came close to disappearing.

That changed with the 1985 release of the Nintendo Entertainment System (NES). Thanks to its colorful graphics and wide variety of unique and interesting games, the NES became the most successful home console of its time.

Designer Shigeru Miyamoto led the development of some of the NES's greatest games. Miyamoto's *Super Mario Bros.* became one of the console's earliest and biggest hits. The game's hero, Mario, soon became Nintendo's mascot. He has appeared in dozens of the company's games. Miyamoto also created the NES hits *Donkey Kong* and *The Legend of Zelda*, which continue to rank among Nintendo's most successful series today.

ON THE GO

In addition to its success with home consoles, Nintendo was a pioneer in the world of handheld video game systems. Its earliest efforts were the Game & Watch systems designed by Gunpei Yokoi. Each system contained a single built-in game. Some had two screens and could fold closed, just as the modern DS and 3DS systems can. First released in 1980, Nintendo continued to produce new Game & Watch systems until 1991.

In the meantime, Yokoi was hard at work on his next handheld innovation. Released in 1989, the Game Boy was a full-featured portable console with a cartridge slot and a button layout that was almost identical to that of the NES controller. Though the original model was large and had a screen that could only display four shades of green, later models were smaller and offered colorful graphics.

POWER LIGHT

SCREEN COULD ONLY DISPLAY
FOUR SHADES OF GREEN

SUPER MARIO LAND WAS
ONE OF THE MOST POPULAR
GAME BOY GAMES.

Nintendo has sold almost 119 million Game Boys since introducing the system in 1989.

SPEAKER

14

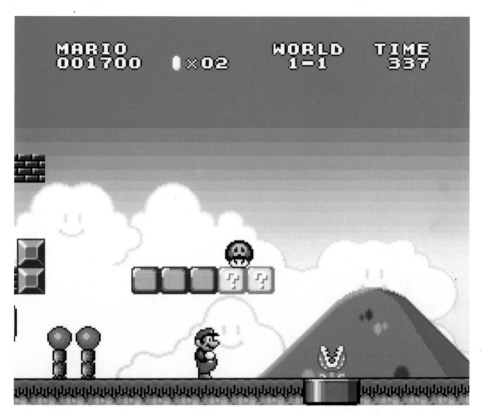

SNES games such as Shigeru Miyamoto's Super Mario World *could display far more colors at a time than NES games could.*

THE 16-BIT ERA

In 1989, Japanese game company Sega released its Genesis console in North America. The Genesis offered more detailed and colorful graphics than the NES. With hit games such as *Golden Axe* and *Sonic the Hedgehog*, the system caught on and provided Nintendo with its first serious competition in the home console market. In 1991, Nintendo fought back by releasing the Super Nintendo Entertainment System (SNES), which matched the Genesis's graphics and sound capabilities and came packaged with the latest game in the popular Mario series. For the next several years, Nintendo and Sega competed for dominance, and both systems turned out to be enormously successful. Video games were more popular than ever before.

A NEW CHALLENGER

In 1995, Sony entered the console business with its PlayStation system, which offered advanced three-dimensional (3D) graphics and CD-quality music. Because PlayStation games came on CDs instead of cartridges, they cost less than games for other consoles. Gamers were wowed by the impressive new technology and inexpensive games, and the PlayStation was an immediate success. Some of its biggest hits included SquareSoft's role-playing classic *Final Fantasy VII* and Capcom's zombie-filled *Resident Evil*.

That same year, Sega released the Saturn, its follow-up to the Genesis. However, the new system lacked impressive games and was considered a flop.

The following year, Nintendo countered with the Nintendo 64. The system's popular new Super Mario title featured groundbreaking 3D graphics and innovative gameplay, and the adventure epic *The Legend of Zelda: Ocarina of Time* offered a huge game world to explore.

RESET BUTTON

POWER BUTTON

MEMORY CARD SLOT

BUTTON TO OPEN DISC LID

Before releasing its PlayStation console in 1995, Sony had worked with Nintendo to create a CD-based add-on for the SNES that was never released.

Super Smash Bros. Melee *was among the most popular games released for Nintendo's GameCube console.*

THE NEXT GENERATION

Sony's PlayStation 2 was released in 2000. With its built-in DVD player and ability to produce high-quality sound, it was advertised as not just a video game console, but a complete home entertainment system. These features changed the way people thought about game systems and made the PS2 a hit with older audiences. Developers began to create more games that would appeal to adults.

The following year, the computer giant Microsoft released its first game console, the Xbox. Like the PS2, Xbox offered the ability to play DVDs and listen to music. It also offered several features common on computers but new to game consoles, such as easy Internet access and a built-in hard drive for saving game progress.

Nintendo's GameCube console hit the market just days after the release of the Xbox. It was the first Nintendo console to abandon cartridges. Instead, its games came printed on discs that were much smaller than CDs or DVDs. As a result, the system could not play DVDs like its competitors could.

PAST MARVELS

The online services of the Dreamcast paved the way for the later success of Xbox Live.

GOING ONLINE

In 1998, Sega released its Dreamcast console. The Dreamcast included a **modem** to allow online gaming, a first for consoles. Players around the world could go online to cooperate or compete in games such as *Quake III Arena* and *ChuChu Rocket!* While this is a common feature of today's game consoles, it was a major innovation at the time of the Dreamcast's release.

PHANTASY STAR ONLINE

One of the most popular online games for the Dreamcast was *Phantasy Star Online*. Part of Sega's popular *Phantasy Star* series of role-playing games, it allowed players to team up in groups to fight monsters, collect new weapons, and make their characters grow stronger. Versions of the game were later created for Xbox, GameCube, PlayStation Vita, and iOS devices.

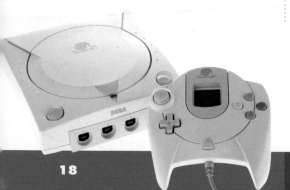

The Dreamcast Visual Memory Unit could be plugged into a controller and used to display extra data while playing games.

ADDING ON

While today's games make use of voice chat to help players communicate online, most Internet connections during the time of the Dreamcast were not fast enough to transmit players' voices without delays. Instead, players relied on text chats to plan strategies and chat about their games. Sega released keyboards and mice like those of a desktop computer to make typing these messages easier.

Later in the console's life span, Sega released an add-on that enabled players to take their Dreamcasts online using a faster broadband connection instead of a modem. The 2001 game *Alien Front Online* took advantage of the faster Internet connection and the Dreamcast's microphone, enabling console gamers to voice chat online for the first time.

The Dreamcast featured impressive 3D graphics that were a step up from its competition on the PlayStation and Nintendo 64.

AN UNHAPPY ENDING

Sega had a success story after its failure with the Saturn. The company eventually sold 10 million Dreamcast consoles. But Dreamcast sales collapsed when Sony announced the PlayStation 2. The Dreamcast failed to save the company. Sega left the console business in 2001. However, the Dreamcast still enjoys a strong reputation among those who played its games.

AHEAD OF ITS TIME

Though the Dreamcast was not the hit Sega needed it to be, its influence soon spread to other game consoles. Microsoft's Xbox offered a built-in connection for broadband Internet. Sony's PlayStation 2 also allowed online play, though early models of the console did not have this functionality built in. Instead, players had to purchase a separate network adapter device and plug it into the back of the system. ☀

19

At the annual Electronic Entertainment Expo, commonly known as E3, thousands of people gather for a chance to check out the latest games months before they are released.

CHAPTER TWO

THE LATEST AND GREATEST

Many science fiction writers once spun mindbending tales of realistic **virtual** worlds. People found the idea of escaping into a computer-generated setting just as unbelievable as time travel or UFOs. But thanks to modern video game technology, those stories have become reality. The creators of video game hardware and software draw players into complex game worlds through cutting-edge control schemes, jaw-dropping sound, and eye-popping visuals. When you play the latest games, you can easily find yourself stepping into a virtual experience so detailed that it seems real.

FAMOUS FAILURES

1982	1992	1994	1995	1999
E.T. the Extra-Terrestrial is released for the Atari 2600 console and fails both critically and commercially, losing millions of dollars for Atari.	Sega attempts to improve the Genesis with a CD-based add-on, but a lack of quality games keeps it from succeeding.	Sega releases another Genesis add-on called the 32X, but it sells even worse than Sega CD.	Nintendo's Virtual Boy console attempts to provide one of the first 3D experiences, but sells under a million units.	Superman is released for Nintendo 64 and quickly develops a reputation as one of the worst video games ever made.

GIVING GRAPHICS A BOOST

Microsoft's Xbox 360 and Sony's PlayStation 3 are the first consoles to take advantage of high definition (HD) televisions, allowing for sharper, more detailed graphics than their predecessors.

Both the Xbox 360 and the PS3 have continued the strategy of turning game consoles into full-featured home entertainment machines. Both are able to play DVD movies, stream music and videos from the Internet, and surf the Internet. The PS3 is also able to play Blu-ray movies. Such features have made the systems popular even among people who do not play many video games.

The Halo *games are among the most popular titles available on the Xbox 360.*

Released in 2007, Nintendo's Wii Fit allows players to exercise using yoga, aerobics, and other techniques. The game tracks each player's workout progress.

A DIFFERENT APPROACH

When Nintendo launched a console to compete with the Xbox 360 and PlayStation 3, it decided to set the new console apart as an entirely different kind of video game experience. It hoped that this approach would pull in new audiences.

SHIGERU MIYAMOTO

In addition to designing many of Nintendo's classic games and coming up with its best-known characters, Shigeru Miyamoto has helped create some of the company's innovative hardware designs, including the Wii. He came up with the idea of the Wii Remote in hopes that it would interest people who had never played video games before. "Our goal was to come up with a machine that moms would want," he said.

That machine was a new console called the Wii. Nintendo's engineers equipped the Wii with sensors that tracked the movement of the Wii's game controller, called the Wii Remote. As intended, the controller encourages new kinds of interaction. Players can do things such as bowl or play tennis by using their own movements rather than just pressing buttons. The Wii's sports and dance games brought millions of new people to video games. Some players even use Wii games for exercise and physical therapy. The Wii proved so popular that both Sony and Microsoft created motion control **peripherals** for their own consoles.

FROM THIS TO THAT

Lego City: Undercover *was one of the Wii U's earliest hits.*

Wii U

In 2012, Nintendo released the successor to the Wii. The new console, called the Wii U, offers advanced HD graphics similar to what the Xbox 360 and PlayStation 3 can produce. Like the previous Wii, it also takes advantage of a unique new control method. The system's gamepad has a large, built-in touch screen in the center.

A SCREEN THAT DOES EVERYTHING

Players can use the touch screen on the Wii U gamepad to help control the action on the big screen. For example, a football game might use the touch screen to display a playbook. Players could then select each play using the touch screen. An adventure game might use the touch screen to display an interactive map to help the player avoid getting lost in a huge game world.

Customers in Osaka, Japan, lined up to purchase Wii U systems when the console was launched on December 8, 2012.

AROUND THE HOUSE

The touch screen also has a second purpose—it can be used to display the games themselves. If a player wants to enjoy a Wii U game, but someone else is using the TV, he or she can simply play the game on the controller's built-in screen. Thanks to the controller's wireless technology, players can even enjoy their Wii U games all the way across the house from their console.

KEEP MOVING

Even though the Wii U is a brand-new console, it makes use of the various controllers from the previous Wii system. This means that players who invested in Wii remotes, gamepads, and other devices can still find a use for them with the latest games. For example, the game *Nintendoland* allows players using Wii remotes and the Wii U gamepad to compete side by side in a variety of fast-paced arcade games. ✴

Wii U's unique controller helped set it apart from the original Wii system.

TOUCH AND GO

With the latest touch screen technology, the action is literally right at players' fingertips. One of the first systems to include touch controls was Nintendo's handheld DS system. The DS features two screens. One is a regular video screen. The other is sensitive to touch from fingers or a stylus. Game designers have used this feature to create a wide variety of unique games for the system.

Apple's iPhone and iPad devices are not specifically designed to be game consoles, but millions of people use these touch screen devices to play their favorite games. Sony's latest handheld device, the PlayStation Vita, also features a touch screen, and Nintendo's Wii U system is the first home console to use touch screens.

Thanks to its low price and simple touch-based gameplay, Angry Birds *has been downloaded by more than half a billion users.*

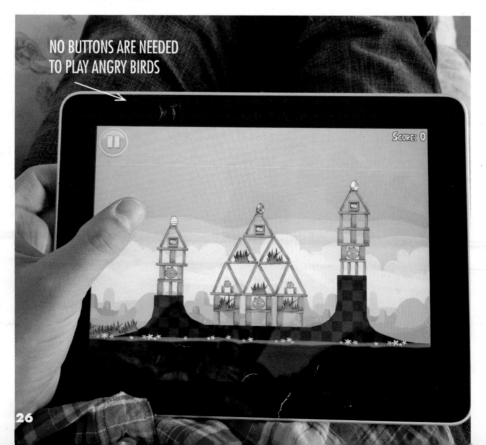

NO BUTTONS ARE NEEDED
TO PLAY ANGRY BIRDS

Many games for the Sony PlayStation 3 allow users to play in 3D using special televisions and glasses.

NEW DIMENSIONS

3D movies have existed for decades. Moviegoers can wear special glasses that make images seem as if they are popping out of the screen. Modern 3D HDTVs allow people to bring the 3D experience home to their living rooms. Microsoft and Sony have both strived to make their game consoles work with these TVs so users can play games in 3D. Both the Xbox 360 and the PS3 offer a variety of 3D-capable games.

Nintendo's handheld 3DS console is an entire system built around the concept of 3D. Unlike 3D TVs, the 3DS does not require users to wear special glasses. Instead of making it seem as if objects are popping out of the screen, it makes it look like the graphics are moving away from the viewer and into the screen. This creates a 3D effect. Users can adjust the strength of the 3D effect by moving a slider on the side of the console.

FROM THIS TO THAT

The twisting knob controllers of early Atari consoles were good for playing the simple games of the time.

IN CONTROL

Game controllers have come a long way over the years. Early controllers were often boxy and had few buttons, limiting the types of possible games. Today's controllers are light and comfortable to hold, with a variety of buttons and joysticks that enable precise control in a wide range of game styles.

TWISTING THE NIGHT AWAY

Early consoles such as the Magnavox Odyssey and Pong systems used simple knobs to control the onscreen action. On the Odyssey controller, players twisted one knob to control up-and-down movement and another to control side-to-side movement. *Pong* players only needed to move up or down, so controllers had just a single knob.

JOY TO THE WORLD

Other consoles, such as the Atari 2600, featured joystick controllers, which allowed a wider range of movement. Joysticks also became a common feature on coin-operated arcade game cabinets and were popular among people who played games on PCs.

PRESSING BUTTONS

The NES gamepad changed controllers forever. It featured a cross-shaped four-directional "d-pad" on the left side and four buttons on the face of the controllers. This made it the first controller to assign movement to the left hand and other gameplay activities to the right.

Control sticks became an important part of controllers as 3D games became more popular.

NINTENDO 64

DREAMCAST

PLAYSTATION

Wireless controllers communicate with consoles by sending and receiving electronic signals through the air.

TOGETHER AT LAST

The controller for the Nintendo 64 featured a unique three-handled shape. In addition to the traditional d-pad, face buttons, and shoulder buttons, it featured a small joystick called a control stick. This allowed players to navigate more easily through 3D game worlds. Soon after the release of the N64, Sony countered by launching its Dual Shock controller for the PlayStation. The controller featured two control sticks, enabling players to move a character and adjust the game's camera perspective at the same time. Since then, dual control sticks have become a standard feature of game controllers.

FREEDOM

Game controllers once needed to remain connected to consoles with wires in order to play. Released in 2002, Nintendo's WaveBird GameCube controller was one of the first to offer wireless gameplay. Instead of huddling near their consoles, players could sit up to 20 feet (6 meters) away from them. Later systems, including the Xbox 360, PS3, and Wii, got rid of wired controllers altogether.

ON THE MOVE

After the success of the Nintendo Wii, other game companies were inspired to create their own motion control systems. Sony's PlayStation Move controller works a lot like the Wii, with players controlling the action by moving a special controller around. Microsoft took this idea a step further with its Kinect system. Kinect doesn't require any controller at all! Instead, players simply move their bodies in response to the action onscreen. A special camera responds to these movements and uses them to control the game. ✳

Online services such as Xbox Live enable game players to track each other's progress, send messages, and download new games.

PLAYING WITH FRIENDS

With today's online services, it's easier than ever to sign on and play your favorite games with friends from all over the world. Microsoft's Xbox Live and Sony's PlayStation Network both let players create online profiles to track and compare their game progress with their friends. Players can also send messages and customize their profiles with avatars from their favorite games. You can use these services to keep in touch with your real-life friends or find new ones online. You might even end up making new friends in faraway countries! (Remember to never give out personal information to your online friends.)

Almost all new games released for the Xbox 360 and PS3 feature some sort of online multiplayer mode. Sports, racing, fighting, and shooting games allow players to go head-to-head in competitive action. Others focus on cooperative modes where players team up to battle against computer-controlled foes.

DOWNLOAD IT!

People no longer have to make trips to stores or wait for packages to arrive when they want to play the latest games. Instead, they can simply download new games from their favorite services and start playing right away.

This is known as digital distribution. Xbox Live and PSN both offer these download services. Nintendo also allows users to download games. Valve Software's Steam is the most popular digital distribution service for PC games, and Apple's App Store sells millions of games to iPad, iPhone, and Mac users.

In addition to full games, digital distribution services often offer additional content that players can purchase for their games. For example, a racing game might offer new cars or tracks, and a shooter might offer new levels to play on. Such content is often an inexpensive way for players to get more use out of older games.

Microsoft's Surface tablet comes with a built-in service for buying and downloading games.

TOUCH SCREEN

DETACHABLE KEYBOARD

Will Wright's The Sims and The Sims 2 are the best-selling PC games of all time.

CHAPTER THREE

A TEAM OF EXPERTS

Have you ever reached the end of a game's final level? Once you have destroyed the invading aliens' doomsday weapon, escaped from the zombie-infested laboratory, or completed some other incredible task, the game ends and the credits roll. Countless names scroll across the screen, listing the skilled people who worked together to build the game.

Game development teams include creative people such as designers, artists, and writers. They also include people with business knowledge. Most of all, though, these teams are made up of people with backgrounds in technology, math, engineering, and science. *SimCity* and *The Sims* creator Will Wright studied mechanical engineering, robotics, and architecture before making games. John Romero, a major innovator in first-person shooters, spent years as a computer programmer before striking it big with *Doom* in 1993.

GROUNDBREAKING GRAPHICS

1979	1983	1987	1996	1998
The Namco arcade game Galaxian turns heads with its incredible multicolored graphics.	I, Robot is the first video game with polygonal 3D graphics.	Atari's Lynx system is the first handheld console to display color graphics.	id Software's Quake Engine is released, breaking new ground in the rendering of 3D graphics.	The first version of Epic Games' Unreal Engine is released. Updated versions are still used widely today.

Developers at the German company Wooga work together to create their games.

BIGGER GAMES, BIGGER TEAMS

Many of the earliest video games were created by very small teams of designers and programmers. The team that built the original version of *Pac-Man* consisted of only three people: one person to design the game, one to program it, and one to create sound and music. Many games, including hits like *Space Invaders*, were even created entirely by individual people who designed and built every aspect of their games from the ground up. Because graphics and sounds were simple, even designers with limited artistic skills could create the levels and characters that appeared on-screen or the beeping noises that played in the background.

While some games are still made by small groups or individuals, it is now far more common for a large team of people to work together. Each team member specializes in a different part of the process. This allows the team to create complex, detailed games.

FEARLESS LEADERS

A lead designer heads each game development project. In some situations, a lead designer comes up with the concept of the game. Other times, he or she is assigned to lead the creation of a sequel to a popular series or create a game based on a movie or television show.

In either case, it is the lead designer's job to oversee the team and make sure the game created is fun and appealing. The designer might be in charge of a team of dozens, or even hundreds, of people. It is his or her job to weigh suggestions from team members and make important decisions about how the game will work. Discussions with team members help a designer choose the best ideas to pursue. While making these decisions, a designer must keep in mind costs, whether the team's plans are technologically possible, and the game's all-important deadline.

Shigeru Miyamoto has served as the lead designer on some of the most popular video games ever created.

SPEAKING A DIFFERENT LANGUAGE

Programmers use their knowledge of computer programming language to turn designers' ideas and plans into actual game software. **Code** written in a programming language tells a game system's hardware what to do. For example, a team of programmers might write code to create a physics engine for a racing game. The engine allows the virtual cars in the game to move and react to collisions just as real cars do. Another team might write code that allows the game to display colorful, realistic-looking explosions or tells the game what to do when an enemy hits a player's character. Everything you see, hear, or interact with while playing a video game is driven by a programmer's code.

Programmers commonly use languages such as C and C++ to build their games.

Chase Toole, an artist at the video game company THQ, creates sketches that are used to plan out the look of game worlds.

BUILDING WORLDS

One of the most important parts of any video game is its virtual world. From the simple 2D side-scrolling levels of *Super Mario Bros.* to the sprawling 3D worlds of today's open-world games, each level in a game must be carefully designed to be both fun to play and fun to explore.

Level designers begin by sketching out ideas. They might use concept art or notes from other team members to help them figure out how each level should look. Drawing a map can help them plot out different points in a level where a player might encounter obstacles or where a hidden area might fit in. Once they know what the level should look like, they use computer software to begin building the actual levels. Many game developers use special level design software built by their own programmers.

Casey O'Donnell is an independent game designer and an assistant professor at Michigan State University. His first game, Osy Osmosis, *was released in February 2011.*

What made you realize that you wanted to design video games?

There were two important moments for me. The first came when playing *Super Mario Bros.* 3 on the Nintendo Entertainment System. There is this moment where if you wait for eight or more Goombas to fall from a pipe, the system slows down. It was the first time I had ever seen a bug in a game—a mistake. I realized then that people make games, that [the games] aren't magic.

The second moment came when playing *Super Mario 64* for the Nintendo 64. I was in college at the time, learning to program and working on the same Silicon Graphics computers that powered the hardware of the Nintendo 64. I looked at what was on the screen and realized I knew how they had done that and perhaps more importantly, that I could do it.

What kinds of projects and jobs did you work on before designing games? How did those activities prepare you for your career?

I worked for NASA's Jet Propulsion Laboratories in Pasadena, California. I was a programmer on a team working on a piece of software that read all sorts of satellite and other data formats. My responsibility was generating different kinds of 3D images from those data sources. The CEO of a game company in La Jolla, California, thought the images were pretty cool and offered me a job.

Which school subjects are most important for budding game developers to study? It depends on your interest. If you want to be an artist, study art, but also take math and programming classes so you understand the computer. If you want to be a designer, take art, English, physics, math, and programming. If you want to be an engineer, take lots of math, physics, and programming classes. Play lots of board games. Play games that aren't just the big games. Play old games. Play a sport. Learn about what makes something fun or not.

Teamwork is an important part of building games. Does working with a group come naturally to you, or is it a skill you've had to develop over time? Teamwork and cooperation are things that everyone can work to improve. I like working with others. Always try to understand other people's perspectives, especially if you disagree with them.

Casey O'Donnell helped create the game Osy Osmosis.

Is there a certain game that you are especially proud of having worked on? *Osy Osmosis* is the first game that I made that I think bridges the gap between mainstream games and educational games. I'm very proud that we were able to build something that is educational and fun at the same time. There are other games that I've been a part of, but this was the first game that started out completely in my head and wound up as a real thing.

If you had unlimited resources to build the game of your dreams, what would it be? The game of my dreams would be a game that players would come away from with a sense of how precious and finite every day of their life is and how important it is to live that life to the fullest. I have no idea how to make that game, but I want to.

What advice would you offer to a young person who wants to design games one day? Never wait for someone to tell you how to do something. Go figure it out yourself. Find people that know what they're doing and ask them for help. Surround yourself with interesting and creative people and learn from them. Read. Try something new as often as you can. Ask lots of question and try to figure out how something works. ☀

Game designers often use sketches to help them plan how 3D models will look.

MAKING MODELS

Even with interesting levels to explore, a game wouldn't be much fun if its world wasn't populated with characters, vehicles, buildings, and other objects. 3D modelers use computer programs to build these things. In a 3D game, everything you see is built from **polygons**. The more polygons an object includes, the more detailed it can be. For example, if you look at the character models in a 3D game for the Nintendo 64 or the first PlayStation, you will probably notice that they look pointy or blocky. One of these characters might have been modeled from several hundred polygons. In today's games, on the other hand, a single character model might be built out of tens of thousands of individual polygons.

ON THE SURFACE

A completed 3D model does not quite look like what you see when you play a game. Instead, the figure looks as if it is made out of wires. If you look closely at one of these models, you can see each individual polygon. It is only once **textures** are added to these models that they look finished.

Texture artists are the team members who create the "skins" that cover a 3D model's surface. This might include anything from creating rocky textures that cover a mountainside to creating realistic skin for human characters. Creating these textures can be tricky. Because the textures must wrap around 3D objects instead of lying flat on a surface, the artists have to design skins so they will match up correctly when they are placed on the models.

The colorful surfaces of characters and objects in games such as Epic Mickey 2 *are the work of texture artists.*

To create realistic sports games, game developers use special technology to capture the actual motions of professional athletes. These motions are used to animate the games' 3D models.

MOTION SENSORS

IN MOTION

Animators are in charge of putting 3D models in motion. Today's games have a lot of moving parts, from obvious ones such as characters or vehicles to smaller details such as leaves falling from trees or grass swaying in a breeze. Some of these animations, such as character movements, are a necessary part of the gameplay. Others add visual details that draw the player into the experience. Animators carefully study the way real objects move in the world to learn how 3D models should move in a game. Sometimes they use motion capture technology to assign actual human movements to 3D models. This is especially common in sports games and other video games that feature realistic human characters.

A FOOT IN THE DOOR

Many people working in game development get their start by working as video game testers. Testers play games before they are released to help the development team find bugs, balance difficulty, and search out any other issues that need to be fixed. This helps the developers polish the game and make sure it is perfect before it is released.

Playing video games all day might sound like a fun job, but it is not always as easy as it sounds. Testers often have to play the same parts of video games over and over dozens of times in as many different ways as possible in order to test every possible issue the game could have. However, this experience makes game testing a great training ground for people who want to learn game development from the inside.

Even though game testers get paid to play video games all day, they work very hard at their jobs to make sure each game is as good as it can be.

THE ARTISTIC SIDE

Sound designers use the latest technology to create realistic sound effects for games.

MAKE SOME NOISE

Modern video game systems are capable of outputting high quality sound and music. The voice acting and sound effects in a big budget game are often on par with those of Hollywood movies. These stunning sounds help game designers tell incredible stories and draw players into a game's virtual world. Next time you play a game, turn up your speakers and listen closely to the work of talented voice actors, sound designers, and musicians.

VOICE ACTING

Many modern video games feature elaborate storylines filled with daring heroes, comical sidekicks, and dastardly villains. Professional actors provide the voices of these characters, just like the voices in animated movies. If the game is based on a movie, these actors might be the same people you see up on the big screen. Other times, actors who specialize in voice work perform the voices. Many voice actors can alter their voices to create a variety of different characters.

SOUND EFFECTS

From realistic explosions and engine noises to the electronic sounds produced as players scroll through menus and select options, game developers carefully design and choose each sound effect. Some sound effects are created using computers and **synthesizers**. Expert sound designers search through libraries of noises and alter them electronically until they get the sound they need. Other times, real-life noises are recorded to make the sound effects. For example, a sound effects designer might record the sound of wooden sticks clattering together and use it as the noise made by the rattling bones of a skeleton enemy in the game.

MUSIC

Music has long been a part of the video game experience. Game developers often hire composers to create scores for their games. Sometimes the music is created using synthesizers and other electronic instruments. Other times, a rock band or even a full orchestra performs it. Today, video game music is so popular that huge audiences attend concerts where musicians perform pieces from well-known games.

Not all game soundtracks feature original music. Many feature songs by popular musicians instead. In these situations, a music director works with artists and record labels to decide which songs will appear in the game. ✴

Composer Nobuo Uematsu's video game music is so popular that it is performed at sold-out concerts around the world.

A blockbuster game such as Call of Duty: Black Ops II *costs hundreds of millions of dollars to develop, market, and manufacture.*

4

PUTTING IT ALL TOGETHER

Video game characters are often thrust into situations where they must overcome incredible odds to save the world or prevent some terrible calamity from happening. These soldiers, superheroes, and space pilots face struggle after struggle as the levels progress and the game grows more difficult. The life of a game maker is surprisingly similar. Like the characters they create, video game designers perform heroic deeds and race against the clock to meet seemingly impossible goals.

Creating a video game is a high-stakes investment of time, money, and hard work. Most modern games usually take at least a year to develop, and many take even longer. A game developer might devote several years of his or her life to completing a single game. Creating and **marketing** a successful game also costs a great deal of money. Most major releases cost tens of millions of dollars to make, and even small, independent projects can cost hundreds of thousands of dollars.

FANTASTIC FIRSTS

1952	1972	1988	1993
The first computer game, OXO, is created by A. S. Douglas at Cambridge University.	The first home video game console, the Magnavox Odyssey, is released.	The first CD-based game console, the PC-Engine CD-ROM, is released in Japan.	The first motion-based controller, the Sega Activator, is released.

Jaakko Iisalo is the senior game designer at Rovio Mobile, the studio behind the Angry Birds *series.*

MAKING PLANS

Because it is so expensive and time-consuming to create a video game, developers must be sure that their ideas will make a good game before they devote too many resources to the project. Trying to push forward with a weak idea can be a costly mistake. Before developers begin the process of creating the actual game, they work on a detailed plan. Designers write long documents describing characters, story ideas, levels, and gameplay systems. Artists create drawings and paintings to show what the game's world and characters might look like.

POWERING UP THE ENGINE

Once the developers have a solid plan in place, they can begin dealing with the underlying programs that will power their game. These programs are known as game engines. Engines control everything from the way a game's graphics are displayed to how physics and artificial intelligence work within the game world. Many developers license engines from other companies. This means they pay a certain amount of money to use a prebuilt engine, allowing them to save the time and effort of creating their own. Sometimes they might modify the licensed engines to suit their specific needs.

To create Batman: Arkham City, *Rocksteady Studios licensed Unreal Engine 3, created by Epic Games.*

WHERE THE MAGIC HAPPENS

DIGIPEN

As video games have become more popular, many well-known universities have begun offering degrees in game design. These degrees are usually part of traditional computer science programs. However, DigiPen Institute of Technology in Redmond, Washington, was built from the ground up to teach students the ins and outs of making video games. This cutting-edge school was founded in 1988 as a computer animation company. It began offering training courses for animators in 1990 and soon started working alongside Nintendo of America to develop a program to teach video game design. Four years later, DigiPen accepted its first class of game design students, and it has since become a respected source of new talent for the video game industry.

HANDS ON

DigiPen fully immerses its students in the experience of creating a video game from start to finish. Students form groups and use the knowledge they gain in the classroom to design and build fully functioning games. Sometimes these student projects are so impressive that they get attention from the pros. For example, one team of DigiPen students created a game called *Narbacular Drop* in 2005. The game was based around the idea of creating portals to solve puzzles and move through tricky situations. Valve Software was so impressed with the game that it hired the entire team, who then used the concept of their original project to create the best-selling *Portal* series.

Nitronic Rush *is a futuristic racing game completed by DigiPen students during the 2010-11 school year.*

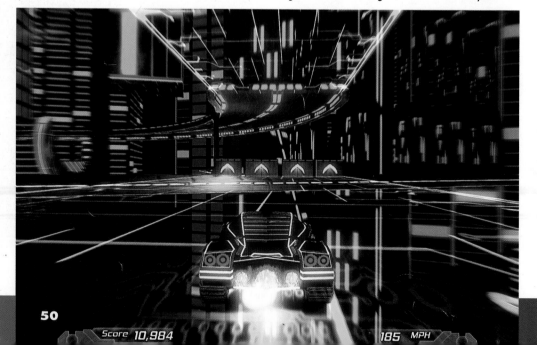

Score 10,984   185   MPH

WELL-ROUNDED

Students at DigiPen earn degrees in such fields as game design, digital art and animation, and computer engineering. But that doesn't mean they don't study other topics as well. Courses in writing and business give them the skills they will need to start game design companies after graduating, while classes in philosophy and psychology help them understand what makes games fun and why people like certain types of gameplay.

NOT JUST FUN AND GAMES

Studying video games can be a lot of fun. After all, what could be better than learning about something you love to do? That doesn't mean that studying at DigiPen is easy, though. Students are expected to work long hours and study challenging subjects. The average school day at DigiPen lasts around 13 hours. About half that time is spent in the classroom, while the other half is spent in a computer lab working on game projects. These long hours give students a taste of what life can be like for professional game developers, who sometimes work very long hours in order to finish games on time.

BE PREPARED

Colleges like DigiPen don't admit just anyone into their programs. Future students need to prove themselves with strong applications before DigiPen will accept them. This means that if you want to study there, you will need good grades in high school, especially in your math and science classes. You also need high ACT or SAT scores and letters of recommendation from teachers or employers. This might seem like a lot of work, but if you truly want to learn the art of game design, the reward will be well worth the effort. ✷

In Terra: The Legend of the Geochine, *a DigiPen student game from 2011, players solve puzzles in a 3D fantasy world.*

Some companies employ huge teams of workers to create assets.

CREATING ASSETS

With an engine in place, designers are free to begin building assets. These are the characters, levels, and other elements that make up the game world. The designers use concept art and design documents as a guide and try to make their creations match the plans as much as technologically possible. The lead designer oversees the process and offers feedback. Creating these game assets can be one of the most time-consuming parts of the entire process, because advanced computer graphics are incredibly detailed.

ADJUSTING IDEAS

As all of the assets come together within the engine, something resembling a completed game begins to take shape. The developers begin to see which of their early ideas work and which do not. They begin to make tweaks and adjust their plans for the game. Sometimes a game can change a great deal during this process. An idea that seemed great on paper might turn out to be frustrating once it is actually a part of the game. Developers might also run into situations where current technology is not powerful enough to make their ideas work properly. Eventually, they will end up with a playable version of the final game. It is likely filled with bugs and might have missing content, but it offers a rough version of what the completed product will look like. This is known as the game's alpha version.

Ed Del Castillo, president of Liquid Entertainment, tests out his company's Facebook-based game Dungeons and Dragons: Heroes of Neverwinter.

LASTING CONTRIBUTIONS

A FLAT WORLD

In the mid-1990s, 3D graphics began to become more popular than 2D graphics. Today, almost all major game releases take advantage of the latest 3D graphics technology, and developers battle to see who can create the most realistic-looking games. However, that doesn't mean 2D graphics have disappeared. Many designers appreciate these graphics because they do not require as much time to create. This makes them especially appealing to small, independent teams. 2D graphics can also be used to achieve beautiful art styles that 3D graphics cannot replicate.

BASTION

The 2011 action-adventure game *Bastion* tells the story of a hero, called the Kid, as he works to rebuild his world after a huge disaster. It uses colorful, hand-painted 2D graphics to achieve a visual style that is unlike any other game. *Bastion* was a major critical success and has sold more than 500,000 copies. In 2012, a version was released for the iPad, bringing the game to a whole new audience.

Bastion was met with rave reviews from video game critics.

The 2D graphics in Rayman Origins led IGN.com to call the game "one of the prettiest and downright pleasing video games ever created."

RAYMAN ORIGINS

In 1995, French game designer Michel Ancel's *Rayman* was released. *Rayman* was a 2D side-scrolling platform game with beautiful cartoon graphics. Its success led to the sequels *Rayman 2: The Great Escape* and *Rayman 3: Hoodlum Havoc.* Unlike the original game, they were made using 3D graphics. But in 2011, the series returned to its roots with *Rayman Origins*, a brand-new game with 2D graphics and gameplay similar to the first game in the series. Critics praised its detailed 2D visuals and strong gameplay.

ANGRY BIRDS

One of the most popular video games of the past several years has been Rovio Entertainment's *Angry Birds*. This addictive puzzle game was originally released for the iPhone in 2009 and has since been ported to several other systems. Like many other smartphone-based games, it features simple, colorful 2D graphics. But its simple appearance has not kept it from success. Millions of people have played the game and its spin-offs, and the game has spawned a variety of licensed products, including toys and soft drinks. ✳

In a public beta test, game fans get a chance to download and play new games before their official release in exchange for helping the development team sort out balance issues and minor bugs.

ON TO THE BETA

The developers continue working on the alpha version to polish it and get it closer to a final product. They replace any temporary art or assets with final versions, fix bugs, and optimize the game so that it runs smoothly. Eventually, they reach a point where the game is almost complete. All of the features and assets are in place, and the game is more or less stable. However, there might still be some bugs or minor balance issues with the difficulty. This version of the game is known as the beta version. Developers often release a portion of the beta version of the game to players to help test for bugs or other issues. Sometimes they release the beta to just a few select people. Other times, they allow anyone to download and play a copy of the beta. In addition to helping them find bugs, this also helps promote the game.

SQUASHING THE BUGS

As reports come in from beta testing, the developers iron out the final bugs and make small tweaks to polish the game. Once this process is complete, they reach a final release version of the game. The game code is sent to a manufacturer so that discs can be created. Graphic designers create cover artwork, and the game company's marketing department advertises the game to players. Finally, on release day, players around the world head to their local game stores or log on to their favorite digital distribution service to buy the game. As these players fire up the game for the first time, the developers head off for some much-needed vacation. Their hard work has paid off, and now it's time to rest up and think of ideas for the next game.

Around 245 million video games are sold around the world each year.

THE FUTURE

THE FUTURE

The year 2013 was big for video games. Microsoft and Sony each released the latest versions of their hugely successful Xbox and PlayStation game consoles. Though these new systems are already impressive, they are only just getting started. Over the next several years, game developers will take advantage of the new features and powerful hardware in these new consoles to create games unlike anything that has ever been seen before.

Microsoft's Xbox One console comes with an updated version of the popular Kinect camera.

XBOX ONE

Microsoft's Xbox One console is the successor to the wildly successful Xbox 360. Its advanced hardware allows it to produce visuals far beyond those of its predecessor. However, updated graphics aren't the only thing the console offers. The Xbox One is designed to work as an all-in-one entertainment system. Users can watch movies and live TV, listen to music, play games, video chat with friends, and surf the Internet using a single device. The system also allows users to control it using hand movements and voice commands. This means people can switch from a live broadcast of their favorite sporting event to an online match in the latest video game with just a quick flick of the hand.

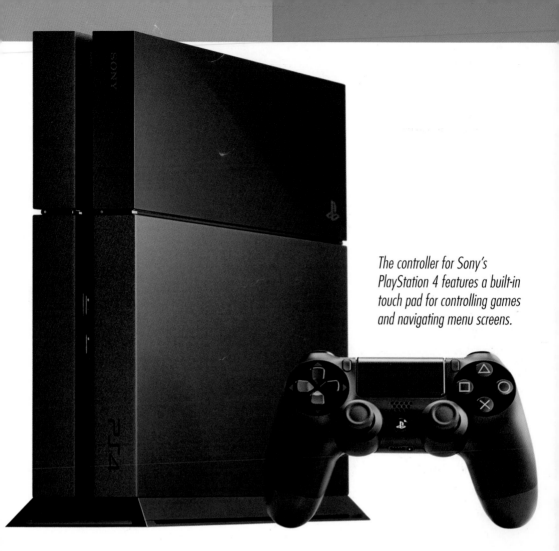

The controller for Sony's PlayStation 4 features a built-in touch pad for controlling games and navigating menu screens.

PLAYSTATION 4

Sony's PlayStation 4 is the most powerful home video game console ever created. Even new systems such as the Xbox One and the Wii U lack the graphic abilities of the PS4.

The PS4 also offers new online features that allow users to interact with their friends as they play. With the press of a special button on the console's controller, users can upload short videos of game footage for their friends to watch. They can also watch friends' videos for tips on playing their favorite games. Combined with text messages and voice chat features, these new options will allow users to play with friends across the globe as if they were sitting together in one living room! ☀

CAREER STATS

SOFTWARE DEVELOPERS

MEDIAN ANNUAL SALARY (2010): $90,530

NUMBER OF JOBS (2010): 913,100

PROJECTED JOB GROWTH: 30%, much faster than average

PROJECTED INCREASE IN JOBS 2010–2020: 270,900

REQUIRED EDUCATION: Bachelor's degree in computer science plus programming skills and experience

LICENSE/CERTIFICATION: Certification may be necessary for certain jobs

PROGRAMMERS

MEDIAN ANNUAL SALARY (2010): $71,380

NUMBER OF JOBS (2010): 363,100

PROJECTED JOB GROWTH: 12%, about as fast as average

PROJECTED INCREASE IN JOBS 2010–2020: 43,700

REQUIRED EDUCATION: Some positions require an associate's degree. Most require a bachelor's degree in computer science, mathematics, or a related field.

LICENSE/CERTIFICATION: Certification may be necessary for certain jobs

MULTIMEDIA ARTISTS AND ANIMATORS

MEDIAN ANNUAL SALARY (2010): $58,510

NUMBER OF JOBS (2010): 66,500

PROJECTED JOB GROWTH: 8%, slower than average

PROJECTED INCREASE IN JOBS 2010–2020: 5,500

REQUIRED EDUCATION: Bachelor's degree in art, computer graphics, computer programming, or a related field

LICENSE/CERTIFICATION: Certification may be necessary for certain jobs

Figures reported by the United States Bureau of Labor Statistics

RESOURCES

BOOKS

Burns, Jan. *Shigeru Miyamoto: Nintendo Game Designer*. Farmington Hills, MI: KidHaven, 2006.

Hot Jobs in Video Games: Cool Careers in Interactive Entertainment. New York: Scholastic, 2010.

Jozefowicz, Chris. *Video Game Developer*. New York: Gareth Stevens, 2009.

Miller, Reagan. *The Economics of the Video Game*. New York: Crabtree, 2013.

Sturm, Jeanne. *Video Games*. Vero Beach, FL: Rourke, 2009.

Thompson, Lisa. *Game On: Have You Got What It Takes to Be a Video Game Developer?*. Minneapolis, MN: Compass Point, 2010.

Wyckoff, Edwin B. *The Guy Who Invented Home Video Games: Ralph Baer and His Awesome Invention*. Berkeley Heights, NJ: Enslow, 2011.

FACTS FOR NOW

Visit this Scholastic Web site for more information on video games:
www.factsfornow.scholastic.com
Enter the keywords **Video Games**

GLOSSARY

code (KODE) the instructions of a computer program, written in a programming language

hardware (HAHRD-wair) computer equipment

marketing (MAHR-kit-ing) the practice of advertising or promoting something so people will want to buy it

modem (MOH-duhm) an electronic device that allows computers to exchange data, especially over a telephone line

peripherals (puh-RIF-uh-rulz) external devices, such as printers or modems, that are connected to and controlled by computers

polygons (PAHL-i-gahnz) shapes with three or more sides; triangles, squares, pentagons, and hexagons are all polygons

synthesizers (SIN-thuh-sye-zurz) electronic keyboard instruments that can imitate the sound of various musical instruments or produce sounds that ordinary instruments cannot

textures (TEKS-churz) the outer layers of 3D models that show how they would feel, such as how rough or smooth they would be

virtual (VUR-choo-uhl) made to seem like the real thing, but created using a computer

INDEX

Page numbers in *italics* indicate illustrations.

INDEX *(CONTINUED)*

ABOUT THE AUTHOR

KEVIN CUNNINGHAM graduated from the University of Illinois at Urbana. He is the author of more than 60 books on history, health, disasters, and other topics. He lives near Chicago, Illinois.